MY YOKE IS EASY

It is for freedom that Christ has set us free. Stand firm, then, and do not let yourselves be burdened again by a yoke of slavery.

Galatians 5:1

FREEDOM AT THE CROSS

My Yoke Is Easy
Copyright © 2016 by Frann Wohlers

All Scripture quotations, unless otherwise indicated, are taken from the Holy Bible, New International Version ®, NIV ®. Copyright © 1973, 1978, 1984, 2011 by Biblica, Inc.™ Used by permission of Zondervan. All rights reserved worldwide. www.zondervan.com The "NIV" and "New International Version" are trademarks registered in the United States Patent and Trademark Office by Biblica, Inc.™

Scripture marked NKJV is taken from the New King James Version ®. Copyright © 1982 by Thomas Nelson. Used by permission. All rights reserved.

Where referenced, scripture quotations are taken from the Holy Bible, New Living Translation, copyright © 1996, 2004, 2007, 2013, 2015 by Tyndale House Foundation. Used by permission of Tyndale House Publishers, Inc., Carol Stream, Illinois 60188. All rights reserved.

No part of this publication may be reproduced without prior permission of the author.

Cover design by David Berkley
Interior design by Dale Jimmo

Printed in the United States of America

Contents

Acknowledgments 1
Foreword 3
Preface 7
Chapter 1 – Come To Me 9
Chapter 2 – Let Us Fix Our Eyes on Jesus 19
Chapter 3 – The Orphan Spirit vs. The Spirit of
   Sonship 25
Chapter 4 – All You Who Are Weary
   and Burdened 37
Chapter 5 – The Framework of the Law
   of Moses 45
Chapter 6 – Context is Critical 53
Chapter 7 – And I Will Give You Rest 61
Chapter 8 – Take My Yoke Upon You 69
Chapter 9 – Only a Shadow 77
Chapter 10 – Learn from Me 83
Chapter 11 – My Yoke is Easy and My Burden
   is Light 91
Chapter 12 – How Then Shall We Live—Aligning
   with God's Heart 99

Acknowledgments

Thank you to my dear husband and partner, Charlie, for your unwavering love, support, and encouragement. Your perspective provided an invaluable balance to mine. My gratitude to my wonderful editor, Jo Ann Memming for the love, joy, peace, gentleness, kindness and patience you consistently express to me. Thank you Elizabeth and Debbie for loving me and teaching me the rock solid foundation of the truth of the scriptures. Many thanks to Liz, Darlene and Kristine—my dear and respected friends—for giving your time, knowledge and perspective to this project.

Foreword

It was like sitting on the front row of a play. As the drama unfolded, I realized I was part of the story and the very hand of God was directing the drama before me. Before the end, what I had witnessed would change my life forever.

For me, this play began in March of 1996 when Frann Wohlers ("Like rollers with a W", I can hear her saying) moved with her husband and two children into my hometown, Jackson, Tennessee. She was an immediate hit. Even so, I can remember feeling a little sorry for her when most introductions included, "So, you're new to the city? Where do you go to church?" She would quickly let it be known she was Jewish, which ended the chitchat. Frann was actually an agnostic Jew even though she had attended Hebrew school as a child and had wonderful memories celebrating the Jewish Feasts with her family in Rhode Island.

At the time the curtain went up on the opening of the drama, I was teaching an interdenominational bible study in Jackson. Frann was invited to attend. I could see the angst on her face each week as she heard the scriptures explained, but she returned week after week. She would be tearful while we sang praises to God. During the teaching I sensed resistance, but then she would go eat lunch with everyone afterward and have a great time. All those around her were amused at God wooing Frann to His heart. Month after month I could personally see Frann moving closer and closer to the bidding of Christ. It became almost comical as Frann would tell about each new friend she had made, each one being a powerful warrior for Christ in the city, unbeknownst to Frann. Little by little you could see Frann's heart softening, but she was still very proud she was a Jew and held firmly to her Jewish roots and traditions.

On November 21, 1997, about twenty months after her arrival, I gathered with others in a room and became an eyewitness to Frann responding to God by calling out to Jesus to be her Messiah and Lord. It was a tremendous turn in the plot.

Frann's excitement and revelation motivated us all. Her insight into the Old Testament narrative provided a solid foundation for deep understanding of New Testament truths. Soon she was teaching me that Jesus was the centerpiece of all the Jewish feasts she had celebrated all those years, but her eyes had been blinded to that revelation until she accepted Jesus. It was only then that I could see this story was more than a Gentile teaching a Jew; it was also a Jew providing valuable insight and knowledge that had been missing in my understanding. God was using each of us to unlock His truths in the scriptures for the other.

I understand I am not called to be Jewish and Frann is not called to be Gentile, but we are gloriously called to be one in Christ Jesus. He destroyed the barriers that once divided and has made us into one body, the church. I am forever changed by this story that unfolded before me and richer for the experience.

Frann and her family moved to Kansas City in August of 2006. Although the curtain closed on our time together in Jackson, she remains my trusted mentor, teacher, and advisor. Her insights have changed my life, and I trust they will do the same for you.

Debbie Currie

Preface

I was born into a Jewish family and was raised under Jewish laws and traditions. Years later, when I became a believer, I understood that I was no longer *under* the laws I was raised with, although I still celebrated some of the festivals and traditions. Yet, I began to meet Gentiles who looked and acted a lot more Jewish than me! I knew Gentiles who attended Torah study on Saturday mornings, kept Kosher, and seemed to know more about the Talmud (teachings and opinions of rabbis central to rabbinic Judaism) than I ever knew. I began to question whether I, a Jew, was doing enough. Perplexed by this phenomenon, I began to research this subject. This book comes as a result of study, seeking the Holy Spirit and searching the truth of the Word of God.

I want to emphatically state that I am not opposed to Gentile believers following Jewish customs and traditions, whether biblical or rabbinic. That is a personal decision. However, there is a big difference between the mindset "I now *choose* to live differently" and the mindset "I now *have* to live differently". Hopefully, this book will provide some clarity.

In recent years, many within the Church have come to realize that the Christian Savior, Jesus Christ, is also the Jewish Messiah, Yeshua HaMashiach. With this revelation, several questions have surfaced among Gentiles regarding how to relate to the Jewishness of Jesus. Questions arise such as, "As a Gentile believer, do I now live differently and if so, what would that look like?" "Do I need to become Jewish?" "Should I now follow Old Testament laws and traditions?" "If so, which ones?" "Where do I go for guidance?" This has become a complex and at times quite controversial topic. It also has the potential to cause divisiveness within the Body of Christ.

At the center of much of the confusion today is the struggle with personal spiritual identity. For all believers--whether Jew or Gentile--our true spiritual identity is in Jesus alone. Everything begins and ends with Jesus and it is in Him where we find everything we need for life and godliness (2 Peter 1:3). God loves Jewish and Gentile believers equally, but we have "separate and unique" identities in the Messiah. True unity in the Body of Christ will come when we understand that although God loves us equally, He never intended for us to look alike. We have been created with unique and distinct roles for His Kingdom purposes.

CHAPTER ONE

Come to Me

I was born in Rhode Island into a Conservative Jewish family. We followed all the Jewish holidays, festivals and traditions. We were a very close and tight knit family and I have wonderful memories of celebrating the holidays together. I went to Sunday school (Jewish children have school on Sunday in synagogue), four years of Hebrew School, and became a Bat Mitzvah, which is a rite of passage for a Jewish girl at age 12. All four of my grandparents had emigrated from Russia at the turn of the 20th century. They brought with them rich Jewish traditions, but also memories of hatred and persecution. I was raised with a mindset: "We Jews have to stick together because the Gentiles cannot be trusted." Where did this mindset come from? My relatives experienced Russian anti-Semitism and the pogroms firsthand. Although they didn't go through the Holocaust, the tragedy of the slaughter of six million European Jews perpetuated the mindset that "the Gentiles hate us."

As a child my world was almost entirely Jewish, but I did go to a public school and had a few Gentile friends. My first personal experience with anti-Semitism came when I was in the first grade. I had a friend named Christopher whom I would play with at school. I had missed two days of school because I was in synagogue to observe the high holy days of Rosh Hashanah. When I came back, Christopher asked me where I had been and when I told him, his response was, "Jewish? You're Jewish? You *can't* be Jewish. You're *nice*, I like you." I was very upset by his comments and when I told my mother about what had happened, she said, "That is why we have to stick together."

When I was a teenager, my parents told me that I could only date Jewish boys. Being a bit rebellious in nature, my first "boyfriend" was Irish Catholic. As a result, my Jewish grandfather, *Zaida*, did not talk to me for 3-1/2 years. I was also taught that because I was Jewish, Jesus was not an option for me. "You can't be Jewish and believe in Jesus." That was the bottom line. Well, I knew I was Jewish, so naturally I could never believe in Jesus. From my perspective, Jesus was only for the Gentiles, and because they couldn't be trusted, neither could He. I was well aware of the long and tragic history of Christian anti-Semitism and what had been done to the Jewish people over the centuries in the name of Jesus.

As a child I wanted to know the God of Israel--the God of Abraham, Isaac and Jacob--that I heard about whenever I went to synagogue. Except for the rabbi in synagogue, I did not hear anyone talking about Him in a way that made Him seem real or personal. By the time I became a teenager, I had pretty much given up on a God who seemed elusive, distant and detached. As I moved into adulthood, God was not on my radar screen. Although I enjoyed many of the Jewish traditions I was raised with, I did not make the connection between my traditions and God. I did not consider Him in regard to anything pertaining to my life.

The "Bible Ladies"

I fell in love with and married Charlie Wohlers, a Gentile who had been raised Catholic but was no longer practicing his faith. While we dated, we came to realize that although we were raised in two different religions, our value systems were the same. We agreed not to "go there" regarding religion. Ten years and two children later, while we were living in Philadelphia, Pennsylvania, Charlie was offered a job promotion in Jackson, Tennessee. I had always supported Charlie's career and told him I would move anywhere with him *except to The South*. As a Jewish Yankee from Rhode Island who had never lived in The South, I somehow felt threatened by the "bible belt." I just knew that I would finally meet those Gentiles I had heard about from my parents and grandparents.

Ultimately, I did not want to hinder Charlie's career and agreed that he should take the job in Tennessee. At the time we moved to Jackson, I believed I was a woman who had it all, and from the world's perspective it was true. I had a wonderful husband and marriage, two beautiful and healthy children, and financial security. In my not-so-humble opinion, I owed it all to myself and the wise decisions I had made.

Not long after we arrived in Jackson, I began to meet women and make new friends. Looking back, it was as though God was surrounding me with born-again believers. At first, I was completely unaware of the fact that most of them were Christians, but as I got to know them I learned that they loved Jesus. Then I began to learn something that was completely contradictory to what I had always believed--these women not only loved Jesus, they also loved the Jewish people. How could this be? Christians who loved the Jews? I knew the long and tragic history of what had been done to my people throughout Christian history in the name of Jesus. But, there it was--these women loved Jesus AND the Jewish people and they were expressing that love to me. I was dumbfounded. I was expecting to finally meet "those Gentiles who were against the Jews," but I was experiencing the very opposite!

God continued to surround me with more and more born-again friends. I called them "The Bible Ladies." After awhile, I began to realize that they had something I didn't. I was a woman who thought she had it all, and yet there was something about these women that was different and magnetic. Although it sounds like a cliche, the truth is they had a love, joy and peace that I had never experienced before, and they were extending that love to me--a Jewish woman!

I was invited to a bible study and being a very open-minded person I thought, "Why not? I'll try anything once." Little did I know that all I would hear about was Jesus--Jesus, Jesus, Jesus. I was offended and yet week after week I went back. I would "endure" the teaching about Jesus because afterwards we would go to lunch and the women would love on me and it felt so good. Although I didn't realize it at the time, many seeds were being sown at that bible study.

The more I was around these women, the more I wanted what they had, and they literally began to make me jealous.

Again I ask: Did they stumble so as to fall beyond recovery? Not at all! Rather, because of their transgression, salvation has come to the Gentiles to make Israel envious. Romans 11:11

I remember the first time I read Romans 11:11 with unveiled eyes and realized how completely it described my experience. Because of my (Jewish) rejection of Jesus, these Gentile women were eligible for salvation--to be grafted into the natural olive tree of Israel by faith in the Jewish Messiah (Romans 11:17-21). The love they had was drawing me like a magnet; however I was oblivious at the time that what was drawing me and making me jealous was Jesus in them.

A year after we moved to Jackson I went through a difficult time. Charlie lost the job that had brought us there and I became very fearful and anxious. One day we were driving home from a trip and as Charlie drove I began to think about finding a counselor to talk to about my anxiety. All of a sudden a voice--an *audible* voice--interrupted my thoughts and said the words,

"COME TO ME". The voice had come out of nowhere, and I could hardly believe it, but I *knew* I had heard the words "COME TO ME". I had no box to put it in and I was too embarrassed to tell Charlie about it. I thought about that voice and those words for days.

On the following Monday morning I went to work out at the gym with a couple of friends. At one point one of them was telling a story when suddenly she said, "When God speaks, you'd better listen!" When I heard those words, my heart started to pound and I told them about hearing the voice in the car. "Do you think that could have been God?" I asked. "Yes, Frann," one of my friends replied, "That was God." I began to consider it a possibility. After all, I was raised to believe in the God of Abraham, Isaac and Jacob. A few days later I went to visit my friend Elizabeth who was like a mother and mentor to me. I have never known anyone who more exemplified a life filled with faith, love and the joy of the Lord—a life laid down. Elizabeth loved me well and I felt safe telling her about the voice and what it had spoken. She handed me her bible and asked me to read Matthew 11:28-30:

> *COME TO ME, all you who are weary and burdened and I will give you rest. Take My yoke upon you and learn from Me for I am gentle and humble in heart and you will find rest for your souls. For My yoke is easy and My burden is light.*

As I read these words, they described exactly how I was feeling in the car the day I heard the voice--weary, heavy-laden, burdened. I became convinced that it was the God of Abraham who had spoken the words *"COME TO ME"*. I was ecstatic. There really was a God, and in my time of distress He had audibly spoken.

One day I was talking to a friend about hearing God's voice when she looked me straight in the eyes and said, "You know Frann, that wasn't God who spoke to you in the car, that was *Jesus*." She understood that to me there was a huge difference, but I wasn't buying it. She was not about to burst my bubble with one very offensive statement. I could accept the fact that my friends loved and believed in Jesus because they were Gentiles, but there was no way He was an option for me and no way He had spoken to me. Upset and determined to prove her wrong, I went home, opened up a bible that had been given to me, found Matthew 11:28-30 and as I read I noticed something I hadn't seen when I was with Elizabeth. The words were in RED LETTERS and I understood what that meant—Jesus had spoken those words. My heart immediately sank and I thought, "What am I going to do about this?" I was filled with dread and fear, but greater than fear was my desire for truth. I simply had to know the truth.

One of my Christian friends had given me a bible when I first moved to Jackson. I would bring it to bible study, but never really read it for myself because to me it was a Christian book and I was no Christian. But now I was willing to consider it.

> *Then Jesus said to those Jews who believed Him, "If you abide in My word, you are My disciples indeed. And you*

shall know the truth, and the truth shall make you free. John 8:31-32 NKJV

I didn't know the truth, but I was about to find out. For the first time, I began to read the bible in earnest. I started in the Old Testament in the book of Genesis—a safe place for me to begin. As I continued to read through the Old Testament, I began to see Jesus everywhere. I was then ready to move into the gospels and before I ever finished the Book of Matthew, I found myself falling in love with Him. I started to realize that He was the "missing link" for that little Jewish girl who was looking for God but could not find Him.

I am the way, the truth and the life. No one comes to the Father except through Me. John 14:6

Accepting Jesus as my Jewish Messiah, however, was a totally different matter and it didn't happen overnight. I began to count the cost. There were many obstacles and hurdles to overcome, not the least of which was how my Jewish family would respond. I knew it would not go well with them, and I feared total rejection from them. But now I realized Jesus was the truth and that there was no turning back. Five months after hearing His voice in the car, I had counted the cost, found Him more than worthy, and gave my heart and my life to my Messiah, Jesus.

And everyone who has left houses or brothers or sisters or father or mother or wife or children or fields for My sake will receive a hundred times as much and will inherit eternal life. Matthew 19:29

For many years I thought about Matthew 11:28-30 only from the perspective of Jesus calling me to follow Him. After all, the only words He had spoken were *"COME TO ME."* It wasn't until years later that I realized Jesus was also telling me something else very significant in those words. But, more about that later (See chapter 8).

After ten years in Jackson, a new job for Charlie relocated us to Kansas City. It was there that I encountered something new--Gentile believers who not only loved Israel and the Jewish people but who were also embracing Jewish laws, customs and traditions to varying degrees. On the one hand, it was such a blessing to meet so many who loved and supported Israel, but there were times when I felt an uneasiness with the degree to which many were immersing themselves in all things Jewish.

Notes

CHAPTER TWO
Let Us Fix Our Eyes on Jesus

Where did this explosion of interest come from? Traditionally, the belief that God is pretty much done with the Jewish people has been the view of the Church. The Israelites are often referenced as a people who sinned, rebelled and rejected Jesus. As a result, many believe that the Church has replaced Israel as God's chosen and elect. If you want to know what NOT to do, just take a look back at the Israelites' behavior in the Old Testament. In recent years, the revelation has come to some within the Church that God is *not* done with Israel, that He covenanted eternally with them to be their God, that He sovereignly chose them for His purposes, and that He has an end-time plan for them that continues to unfold.

As people begin to read scripture through a new lens--that the Jewish people have always been and will always be God's covenantal people--the question becomes, "Why have I never seen or heard this before?" A natural reaction is to study the Old Testament and the Hebraic roots of the faith with a new set of eyes and understanding. I was entering a new family when I married Charlie and wanted to learn about their customs and traditions. It's natural as people begin to see Jesus as the *Jewish Messiah* that they desire to learn about *His* family, customs and traditions. Understandably, they want to know what this means to them and how they should live with this new revelation.

Again, I want to emphatically state that I am not opposed to Gentiles observing Jewish festivals or traditions. Experiencing and celebrating Jesus' fulfillment of the Festivals of the Lord is beautiful and enriching for both Jew and Gentile. Whatever honors and draws us closer to Him is always beneficial. My uneasiness, however, results from the phenomenon of some Gentile believers steeping themselves in those traditions, then coming to believe it is *necessary* to follow them. What begins as a genuine desire to learn and understand the roots of the faith in some instances evolves into a need to follow rules and regulations--the very rules and regulations Jesus died to set us free from. The very heart of this book deals with why Jesus had to die to set us free from these rules and regulations we could never keep in the first place. I will expand upon what comprises these rules and regulations in Chapters 4 and 5.

When I ask Gentiles why they follow Jewish laws and traditions, one answer often is, "I want to be more pleasing to God." Jesus alone was the perfect sin offering, *fully pleasing to God* (Isaiah 53:10*)*, and fully meeting the requirements we never could. He sets us free from the Law of Moses, which Paul calls the law of sin and death. The works of the flesh, which come from the law, do not make us righteous and do not please

God. Our faith in Him who sets us free is what pleases God.

> ...*because through Christ Jesus the law of the Spirit of life set me free from the law of sin and death. For what the law was powerless to do in that it was weakened by the sinful nature, God did by sending His own Son in the likeness of sinful man to be a sin offering. And so He condemned sin in sinful man, in order that the righteous requirements of the law might be fully met in us, who do not live according to the sinful nature, but according to the Spirit. Romans 8:2-4*

Without *faith* it is impossible to please God (Hebrews 11:6). The scriptures state four times that the righteous will live by *faith* (Habakkuk 2:4, Romans 1:17, Galatians 3:11, Hebrews 10:38). Scripture is clear—Jesus is enough and we don't need to do more than put our faith in Him. After Jesus had fed the five thousand and walked on the sea, the people asked Him in John 6:28, "What shall we do, that we may work the works of God?" Jesus responded:

> *"This is the only work God wants from you: Believe in the One He has sent." John 6:29 NLT*

Jesus must have preeminence in our lives. Preeminence comes from the Greek word *proteuo*, which means, "to be first in rank or influence." In order for Jesus to be preeminent, He must be held in highest esteem in our lives—He must come first. Paul wrote to the Colossians that Jesus is the exact likeness of God, He created everything in the universe, and He holds everything together. As Lord over all creation, He is worthy of first place in all things.

> *He is the image of the invisible God, the firstborn over all creation. For by Him all things were created that are in heaven and on earth, visible and invisible, whether thrones or dominions or principalities or powers. All things were created through Him and for Him. And He is before all things, and In Him all things consist. And He is the Head of the body, the church, who is the beginning, the firstborn from the dead, that in all things He might have the preeminence. Colossians 1:15-18 NKJV*

When we fix our eyes on the right thing, our Messiah, we will victoriously run the race until we reach the finish line of heaven.

> *Let us run with perseverance the race marked out for us,* fixing our eyes on Jesus, *the pioneer and perfecter of faith. For the joy set before Him He endured the cross, scorning its shame, and sat down at the right hand of the throne of God. Hebrews 12:1b-2*

Notes

CHAPTER THREE

The Orphan Spirit vs. The Spirit of Sonship

Even though I am not opposed to Gentiles observing the Festivals of the Lord or any Jewish traditions for that matter, still there are three things that are of concern.

1. The first is when voluntary observance of the traditions turns into the belief that it is *required*. The observance transitions from something I *choose* to do to something I *must* do to please God. This becomes seeking righteousness through our works (self-righteousness) and not through faith. It says that Jesus' death wasn't enough to satisfy God and there is more *we* must do.

2. The second concern is when Gentiles try to find their *identity* in Jewish traditions and works of the law. This sometimes comes as the result of an "orphan spirit." When we live out of an orphan spirit, we do not find our *true* identity as children of God.

Adam and Eve sinned and were alienated from God the Father, and an orphan spirit entered the earth.

Our sin alienates *us* from God, turns us into orphans and robs us of our inheritance. In John 14:18 Jesus tells us, "I will not leave you as orphans." Jesus came to restore our true identity (Sonship) and our inheritance.

> *The thief comes only to steal and kill and destroy; I have come that they may have life and have it to the full. John 10:10*

Satan comes to disconnect us from the Father and steal our inheritance. When we are born again, Jesus restores our relationship to God as our Father and we are no longer orphans. In giving us *life to the full,* He restores our inheritance. However many believers are living as orphans, disconnected from God and their inheritance. According to the author Jack Frost:

> *The orphan spirit causes one to live life as if he does not have a safe and secure place in the Father's heart. He feels he has no place of affirmation, protection, comfort, belonging or affection. Self-oriented, lonely, and inwardly isolated, he has no one from whom to draw Godly inheritance. Therefore, he has to strive, achieve, compete, and earn everything he gets in life. It easily leads to a life of anxiety, fears, and frustration.*

An orphan spirit is characterized by a sense of abandonment, loneliness, alienation and isolation. God did not create mankind to be abandoned, lonely, alienated and isolated! God created mankind for two reasons: Sonship and inheritance.

> *Then God said, "Let us make mankind* in our image, in our likeness, so that they may rule *over the fish in the*

sea and the birds in the sky, over the livestock and all the wild animals, and over all the creatures that move along the ground." Genesis 1:26

In our image, in our likeness speaks of a parent/child relationship. *So that they may rule* speaks of an inheritance. We were created to be sons and daughters of God. God gave the whole earth to mankind as an inheritance. Sonship and inheritance were God's plan for us all along.

When we try to find our *identity* through Jewish traditions and works of the law, we are operating out of an orphan spirit. We lose our true identity as sons and daughters of God. The Holy Spirit speaks to our spirit about our true identity and what we have received — the Spirit of Sonship. It is who we are in Jesus. All we have to do is receive and believe that truth by allowing the Holy Spirit to replace our orphan spirit with the spirit of Sonship. It is the work of the Holy Spirit in our lives that reconnects us to the truth of who we are, whose we are and the inheritance we have as sons and daughters of the living God.

> *For those who are led by the Spirit of God are the children of God. The Spirit you received does not make you slaves, so that you live in fear again; rather, the Spirit you received brought about your adoption to Sonship. And by Him we cry "Abba, Father." The Spirit Himself testifies with our spirit that we are God's children. Now if we are children, then we are heirs — heirs of God and co-heirs with Christ, if indeed we share in His sufferings in order that we may also share in His glory. Romans 8:14-17*

In Jesus, we are *all* sons and daughters of God. At the same time, it is important that Jews and Gentiles understand that they each have a unique role and divine purpose. If Gentiles look no different than the Jewish people, our distinct roles and purposes become blurred. A true "one new man" (Ephesians 2:15-16) will emerge when we understand our unique roles in God's plan.

The Jewish Role:

God chose Israel to create a context in which He could be clearly seen and known in order to reveal His character and deeds to mankind. Israel was called to be a light and a witness to the Gentiles.

Time and time again God showed His faithfulness to a rebellious people who have survived against impossible odds. After more than 1900 years in exile, the Jewish people are back in the land of Israel; the Hebrew language is once again spoken; and the land is now flourishing as God promised it would when His people returned. All this is evidence of God's faithfulness to the covenant promises He made with Israel.

> *"And I will bring My people Israel back from exile. They will rebuild the ruined cities and live in them. They will plant vineyards and drink their wine; they will make gardens and eat their fruit. I will plant Israel in their own land, never again to be uprooted from the land I have given them," says the Lord your God. Amos 9:14-15*

Through the Jewish prophets, the disciples and the apostle Paul, God gave the scriptures to the nations.

There are now approximately 2.2 billion Christians worldwide, which would have been impossible without the Word of God.

In His sovereignty God chose to bring salvation to the world through the Jewish bloodline as He became flesh and dwelt among us—our Emmanuel. Jesus died and rose and will return--but not as an atoning sacrificial lamb. He will return as a mighty warrior King, who with justice will judge and make war with His enemies.

> *I saw heaven standing open and there before me was a white horse, whose rider is called Faithful and True. With justice He judges and makes war. Coming out of His mouth is a sharp sword with which to strike down the nations. "He will rule them with an iron scepter." He treads the winepress of the fury of the wrath of God. On His robe and on His thigh He has this name written: KING OF KINGS AND LORD OF LORDS. Revelation 19:11,15-16*

The mighty King of Kings *is* returning, but He will not return until the Jewish people cry out for Him. As Jesus looked out over the city of Jerusalem, He spoke these words to His Jewish brethren, "For I tell you, you will not see Me again until *you* say, 'Blessed is He who comes in the name of the Lord'" (Matthew 23:39). This crucial role of the Jewish people is a necessary pre-condition of Jesus' return.

The Gentile Role:

Gentiles have unique and specific roles to play in God's plan. We learn in Romans 11:11-12 that because the majority of Israel rejected the gospel, salvation is available to the Gentiles *in order to make Israel envious*. When believing Gentiles provoke the Jewish people to jealousy, Israel's fullness (salvation) will bring unprecedented blessing and riches to the world (Romans 11:11-12). Gentiles do not make the Jewish people envious if they look no different. The point is not that Gentiles *become* Jewish to provoke the Jews, it's the love of Jesus in them that will do it.

Consider that both male and female are made in God's image, yet they each have different roles. When they come together in marriage, the two become one, yet their distinct roles remain. The husband is the head, provider, and protector of the wife. The wife is the helpmate to her husband, the child bearer and nurturer. The two become one, but God doesn't want the man to become the woman nor the woman to become the man. It is the same with Jews and Gentiles—God has purposed that they have come together as "one new man" through Jesus' death on the cross. They have peace with one another and they have equal access to the Father by one Spirit. They are "one" in Jesus yet their distinct roles remain. God loves them both equally, but He does not want the Jew to become a Gentile, nor does He want the Gentile to become a Jew.

For He Himself is our peace, Who has made both one and has broken down the middle wall of separation, having

> *abolished in His flesh the enmity, that is, the law of commandments contained in ordinances, so as to create in Himself one new man from the two, thus making peace, and that He might reconcile them both to God in one body through the cross, thereby putting to death the enmity.*
> *Ephesians 2:14-16 NKJV*

A few years ago I met a Gentile woman who had been studying and taking Jewish roots classes for several years. We had a conversation the day we met and she began telling me all the things she knew about Jewish roots and the Torah. Although she knew I was Jewish, she never asked me one thing about myself, nor my opinion about what we were discussing. There she was, a Gentile, telling me, a Jew all about the Jewish people. I listened to her for about an hour and then asked her why she was wearing a Jewish star necklace. She said, "I want to show the Jewish people that I love them." I asked her if she knew any Jewish people. She said the only Jewish person she knew was the Messianic rabbi who facilitated the classes she was taking.

I tried to explain to her that simply wearing a Jewish star would not show love to the Jewish people, in fact it might even offend some. Personally, I was not "feeling the love"! She had a lot of knowledge *about* Jewish people, but she had no interest in me personally or in pursuing a relationship with me—a Jewish person! My time with her felt cold and disconnected. Wearing Jewish jewelry or attire will not provoke a Jew to jealousy, but the love of Jesus will. That is the very thing that drew me to Him—others expressing His love to me. Love *never* fails. With the understanding of God's covenantal promises and faithfulness to Israel, Gentiles have a responsibility to support the Jewish people, pray for their salvation, and love them--but loving them does not mean becoming them.

Although Jesus originally gave the Great Commission to eleven Jewish disciples (Matthew 28:16-20), the gospel continued to dramatically spread as a result of Paul's ministry to the Gentiles. There are now approximately two billion Christians worldwide, which would have been impossible without the Gentile Church evangelizing the gospel throughout the world. Throughout history, as Jews and Gentiles have evangelized the world, God's desire that every nation, tribe and tongue know Him is being fulfilled.

Our True Identity

Although Jews and Gentiles have distinct roles, our true *identity* as sons and daughters of God is found in the Messiah. ***In Him:***

- We are "one new man reconciled to God through the cross" (Ephesians 2:14-15)
- We are God's children and co-heirs with Christ as we share in His sufferings and His glory (Romans 8:17)
- We have been brought to fullness (Colossians 2:10)

- We are holy and blameless in His sight (Ephesians 1:4)
- We are God's workmanship, created in Christ to do good works (Ephesians 2:10)
- We are new creations (2 Corinthians 5:17)
- We are alive to God (Romans 6:11)
- We are more than conquerors (Romans 8:37)
- We are over-comers (Revelation 12:11);
- We are partakers of His divine nature (2 Peter 1:3-4)
- We are Christ's ambassadors (2 Corinthians 5:20)
- We are a chosen people, a royal priesthood, a holy nation, and a people belonging to God (1 Peter 2:9)
- We are the righteousness of God in Jesus (2 Corinthians 5:21)
- We are the temple of the Holy Spirit (1 Corinthians 6:19)
- We are the salt of the earth and the light of the world (Matthew 5:13-14)
- We are rescued from the dominion of darkness (Colossians 1:13)
- We are raised up with Jesus and seated in heavenly realms (Ephesians 2:6)

The list goes on. What a blessing, honor, and privilege. We have a magnificent identity in Jesus and there is no need to look elsewhere. When we have confidence in our true identity in Jesus, we will fulfill not only our *individual* roles, but also our *corporate* destiny that God has established.

3. The third concern is when the study of Hebraic roots shifts the *focus* away from Jesus. This shifting of focus often happens gradually and subtly, and this is where I believe many fall into deception.

A friend of mine shared a story of a missionary in Afghanistan. When this missionary was a new believer, she attended an end-times conference. Being a new believer, she had never heard the things being taught and she became anxious. She asked the Lord, "How do I keep from being deceived?" The Lord gave her an open vision right there in the church. She saw Jesus walking and she was walking directly behind Him. He wore a long white robe and was surrounded by light. As she stayed very close and kept her eyes on Him, she also walked in the light. All of a sudden, she heard voices calling to her on her left side. She turned to look and saw black shadowy figures behind a clear plexiglass wall. As she turned to look at them, the plexiglass wall went down and the black shadowy figures began to reach out and try to pull her into the darkness. She immediately turned her gaze back to Jesus and the plexiglass wall went up and she was protected. She continued to follow Jesus and once again she heard voices calling to her--this time on her right side. She turned to look and saw the same exact scene--black shadowy figures calling to her. Once again, as she took her gaze off Jesus, the plexiglass wall went down and the black shadowy figures tried to pull her into darkness. Immediately she turned her gaze back to Jesus and she was protected once again. Then the Lord spoke and said, "Walk close to ME, keep your eyes on ME and you will not be deceived."

We are living in days when we can all be deceived, and the problem with deception is we don't realize we're deceived! When we put anything ahead of Jesus, when we look elsewhere for our identity, or when anything else becomes our focus or obsession, we open ourselves up to being deceived.

Notes

CHAPTER FOUR

All You Who Are Weary and Burdened

Often, as people begin to dig into Hebraic roots, questions arise. One of the main questions is, "Now that I have this new revelation, how am I as a Gentile to live? Should I change how I live and incorporate Jewish traditions and laws? If so, how many laws and traditions must I follow? Must I now observe Sabbath on Saturday instead of Sunday? Can I drive, work, use electricity, or go shopping on Sabbath? What about the Festivals? Do I observe all of them and, if so, what does that look like? Must I now observe kosher dietary laws? (See chapter 10, Clean and Unclean). Do I have to eat 100% animal fat free? (Leviticus 3:17) Can I no longer eat my meat rare because the law states I cannot eat the blood of any animal? How can I buy fruit from a store if I don't know whether the growers waited five years before selling? (Leviticus 19:23-25) Is it enough if I only abstain from pork and shellfish? The law says I must put my child to death if he curses me (Leviticus 20:9). Leviticus 20:13 commands that I must support the killing of gays and lesbians. Which rules and regulations am I obligated to observe and which ones not?

Who decides? Do I arbitrarily decide? Where do I go to get answers to all my questions? Do I go to a rabbi for guidance? Do I ask a Messianic Jew? Perhaps I should go to Gentiles who have more understanding than me and let them decide for me. These few questions are only the tip of the iceberg. How much is enough? Without even realizing it, we can become weary and burdened by the weight of it all. Let's begin to find the answers by going back to when God gave Moses the Law.

The Ten Commandments and the Law of Moses

In Genesis 12, God spoke to Abram and promised "I will make you into a great nation." Then in Genesis 17, God again spoke to Abram, whom He renamed Abraham, and promised, "I will make you very fruitful; I will make nations of you and kings will come from you." God also gave the entire land of Canaan to Abraham and his descendants in an everlasting covenant (Genesis 15). But the descendants of Abraham were only 70 people when they entered Egypt (Genesis 46:26-27).

Hundreds of years later as God was preparing to deliver His people out of slavery in Egypt, their numbers had increased to 603,550 men who were 20 years or older, plus women and children (Numbers 1:46). Estimates are that there were between 1-2.5 million Israelites by the time of the Exodus. They had certainly become the great nation that God had promised to Abraham. This was the context in which the Ten

Commandments and the Law of Moses were given—they were given to the promised great nation about to enter the land that God had covenanted to them.

I want to distinguish between the Ten Commandments and the Law of Moses:

The Ten Commandments

The Ten Commandments (Exodus 20:1-17, Deuteronomy 5:6-21) are based on God's holy and eternal nature. The Ten Commandments were inscribed by the finger of God and were SET IN STONE (Exodus 31:18, 32:16). They reflect God's holiness, character, precepts and standards. The Ten Commandments are eternally binding for all people—Jew and Gentile--because they are based on God's holy and eternal nature. The first four commandments reflect man's relationship to God. The last six commandments reflect man's relationship to his fellow man. Although we are bound to the Ten Commandments, we don't always obey them perfectly. There are times, for example, when we covet or times we dishonor our parents. But in Jesus, we repent, we are forgiven, and the slate is wiped clean.

Even though they were first given in the Old Testament, the Ten Commandments are referenced in various places within the New Testament, including Matthew 4:10, 6:9,24, 15:3-4,8-9,19-20, 24:20; Mark 10:11-12,19 Luke 4:8; Acts 15:20, 16:13, 17:29-30; Romans 7:7, 13:9; 1 Corinthians 6:9; Ephesians 4:25, 6:1-3; James 2:8.

The Ten Commandments (Exodus 20, Deuteronomy 5) are considered *Mishpatim*--laws, ordinances and judgments that are ethical, rational, self-evident and intuitively obvious. Mishpatim are laws that would have been obvious even if they were not written in the Torah. God has put them in our hearts and on our consciences. The laws that prohibit murder and theft are two examples of Mishpatim.

> *Indeed, when Gentiles, who do not have the law, do by nature things required by the law, they are a law for themselves, even though they do not have the law. They show that the requirements of the law are written on their hearts, their consciences also bearing witness, and their thoughts sometimes accusing them and at other times even defending them. Romans 2:14-15*

The Law of Moses

The Law of Moses (Book of the Law, Book of the Covenant, Mosaic Law, Sinai Covenant) is the God-given law that Moses wrote in a book. The Law of Moses is found in various places in the books of Exodus, Leviticus, Numbers and Deuteronomy. Below is a general breakdown of where the Law of Moses is contained. These comprise the ceremonial (ritual) laws:

1. The Feasts of the Lord – Leviticus 23

2. The Law of a Set Apart Nation – Leviticus 11-15; 18, 21, Numbers 6

3. The Sacrificial Law – Leviticus 1-10

4. The Civil Law – Exodus 21-23, Deuteronomy 19-26, various others

Moses' law was temporary and was given *"until the Seed had come"*; the Seed was Jesus.

> *What, then, was the purpose of the law? It was added because of transgressions until the Seed to whom the promise referred had come. Galatians 3:19*

The ceremonial or ritual laws contained in the Law of Moses are called Hukkim (decrees). While the Mishpatim are rational, intuitively obvious, and written on our hearts and in our consciences, Hukkim are laws that are not generally obvious. They are observed out of obedience even when the reason is not understood. Maimonides, a rabbi from the middle ages and one of the most brilliant and influential Torah scholars of all time, said of the Hukkim, "There is always a reason for a law, though we may not always be able to discern it." Some examples of Hukkim are laws against wearing wool and linen together, some kosher dietary laws, and laws of the red heifer.

Whereas the Ten Commandments, written by the finger of God Himself, apply eternally to all people, the ceremonial laws applied exclusively to the nation of Israel or anyone who wanted to follow the God of Israel (proselytes). God's covenantal people were about to enter the land of Canaan, and He gave them specific instructions on how to live as holy and set-apart in the midst of paganism. The ceremonial laws (hukkim) were contained within an intricate sacrificial system and included various rituals and observances such as sacrifices, offerings, purifications, remembrances of God's work, and also regulations distinguishing the Israelites from their pagan neighbors (i.e., dietary and clothing restrictions).

The civil or judicial law was Israel's legal system. As with the ceremonial laws, it was given exclusively to the Jewish nation. Included in the civil law were penalties for offenses as well as restitution for those wronged.

There is a specific relationship between the Ten Commandments and the Law of Moses. The Ten Commandments defined sin. The Law of Moses defined the remedy for sin. If an Israelite sinned, he broke God's Law. He then had to make restitution according to the Law of Moses in order to receive forgiveness and be restored to relationship with God (http//www.The-Ten-Commandments.org).

Notes

CHAPTER FIVE

The Framework of the Law of Moses

Blood and Sacrifice

The Law of Moses and its practice were carried out within the framework of the Temple, the Levitical Priesthood operating within the Temple and the Sacrificial System. It could not operate outside this framework that has not existed since 70 A.D. when the Temple was destroyed.

> *If perfection could have been attained through the Levitical priesthood—and indeed the law given to the people established that priesthood--why was there still a need for another priest to come, one in the order of Melchizedek, not in the order of Aaron? For when the priesthood is changed, the law must be changed also. Hebrews 7:11-12*

At the heart of the Law of Moses was the shedding of blood. The very detailed and specific blood sacrifices given to Moses were proof that the shedding of blood was necessary to atone for the people's sin.

> *For the life of a creature is in the blood, and I have given it to you to make atonement for yourselves on the*

> *altar; it is the blood that makes atonement for one's life. Leviticus 17:11*

The Law of Moses was ratified (officially approved) by blood.

> *Then he took the Book of the Covenant and read it to the people. They responded, "We will do everything the Lord has said; we will obey." Moses then took the blood, sprinkled it on the people and said, "This is the blood of the covenant that the Lord has made with you in accordance with all these words." Exodus 24:7-8*

The pouring out of an animal's blood was very intricate. There were blood sacrifices to consecrate the priesthood (Ex. 29:10-21; Lev. 8:1-24; Lev. 9:8-14; Lev. 16:1-14). There were blood sacrifices with the burnt offering (Lev. 1:1-17); with the fellowship offering (Lev. 3:1-17); with the sin offering (Lev. 4:1-35); for the guilt offering where restitution was required (Lev. 5:14-19); and for the cleansing of the nation on the Day of Atonement (Lev. 16:15-22).

The shedding of blood was at the foundation of the entire sacrificial system and was God's provision under the Law of Moses for atonement of sin. It pointed to the ultimate sacrifice that was to come—Jesus freely shedding His own blood to atone for the sin of all.

> *In fact, the law requires that nearly everything be cleansed with blood, and without the shedding of blood there is no forgiveness. Hebrews 9:22*

Apart from the sacrificial system and the priesthood, it is impossible to keep the biblical Law of Moses.

When the Temple was destroyed in 70 A.D., its sacrificial system and priesthood couldn't operate according to the Law of Moses. There was no longer the means to carry out acceptable sacrifices, and without the shedding of blood forgiveness could not be granted. It is interesting to note that not long after Jesus died to atone for our sin, the Temple was destroyed and as a result the Levitical sacrificial system that operated within the Temple ceased.

Rabbis were faced with the reality of Judaism operating without a Temple, and ultimately Rabbinic Judaism became the mainstream form of Judaism. In simplest terms, Rabbinic Judaism encompasses the teachings and writings of Rabbis whose works are compiled in the Talmud.

Biblical Law and Halakhah

There is a difference between *biblical law* --the literal law given to Moses in the bible--and the way Jewish people live today called Halakhah or Jewish Law. Halakhah seeks to preserve the Oral Law, which, according to Jewish tradition, includes all that Moses memorized and learned from God but did not write down. The Oral Law has become synonymous with rabbinic commentary that explains how the laws in the Torah are to be carried out. At the heart of Halakhah are the 613 commandments given to Moses in the Torah (biblical law), many of which can no longer be observed because there is no longer a Temple. It is commonly held within Judaism that without an oral tradition, many of the 613 commandments of the Torah would be incomprehensible.

The word Halakhah is derived from the Hebrew word *halak*, which means "to go, to walk or to travel, the path one walks". Halakhah is the way a Jew is directed to behave in every aspect of life and encompasses civil, criminal and religious law. Halakhah developed as a result of rabbis interpreting, modifying and enacting rules of conduct as conditions and circumstances changed for the Jewish people. It has been ongoing since biblical times.

As rabbinic teachings over the generations increased, they were organized and committed to writing. They were compiled in the Mishnah (2nd and 3rd centuries) and the Gemara (4th and 5th centuries). The Mishnah and Gemara taken together are called the Talmud. Many centuries later (12-13th), new compilations from rabbinic scholars such as Moses Maimonides and Jacob ben Asher were added. Halakhah encompasses the Talmud—rules, regulations and traditions that have been *added to* the Torah--exactly what the scriptures command we NOT do.

> *Do not add to what I command you and do not subtract from it, but keep the commands of the Lord your God that I give you. Deuteronomy 4:2*
>
> *You have let go of the commands of God and are holding on to human traditions. Mark 7:8*

Covenant and Testament

By definition, a covenant is "a contract or binding agreement between two parties with various responsibilities, benefits and penalties." In the bible, it was always God who initiated covenant. In doing so, He made promises to His people. God initiated two covenants with all mankind (Adamic/Edenic and Noahic) and four covenants with Israel (Abrahamic, Mosaic, Davidic and New). Three of the four covenants that God made with Israel are eternal (Abrahamic, Davidic and New).

In the Abrahamic Covenant, God made an *everlasting* covenant with Abraham to be his God and the God of his people *eternally* and to give them the land of Canaan as an *everlasting* possession (Genesis 15, 17). In the Davidic Covenant, He promised David an *eternal* kingdom that would come from David's bloodline (2 Samuel 7, 2 Chronicles 17). He made the New Covenant with the House of Israel and the House of Judah, stating that He would *never* reject them and that He would put His law in their minds and on their hearts (Jeremiah 31). Gentiles are "grafted into" the New Covenant given to Israel; however both Jew and Gentile attain salvation only *through faith in Jesus*. (Romans 11, Luke 22).

The "Old Covenant" referred to in the scriptures is the Mosaic Covenant (Law of Moses). It was a conditional covenant. There were blessings for obedience and punishments for disobedience. Unlike the other three covenants that God gave Israel, the Mosaic Covenant was *not* an eternal covenant.

So the law was our guardian until Christ *came that we might be justified by faith. Now that faith has come, we are no longer under a guardian. Galatians 3:24-25*

There are two main divisions of the bible—39 books called the "Old Testament" and 27 books called the "New Testament." The Old Testament *predicts* the coming Messiah and reveals how the shedding of blood reconciles us to God. The New Testament *reveals* the Messiah and His life, ministry, death and resurrection, and how the shedding of *His* blood reconciles us to God once for all. The Old Testament, also referred to as the Old Covenant, gives the law to Israel. The New Testament, also referred to as the New Covenant, explains that the law revealed sin but could never bring righteousness. Righteousness comes only through faith in Jesus to all who believe (Romans 3:19-20).

Notes

CHAPTER SIX
Context is Critical

God's revelation in scripture is progressive. It is important to read the bible as one book from beginning to end in order to keep God's story in context. What is God saying to us as the WHOLE story unfolds?

The biblical Law of Moses was given to a specific people (Israel), at a specific time (over 3400 years ago), at a specific place (Mt. Sinai) and for a specific purpose. The purpose was to establish the nation of Israel in the context of the specific land they were about to enter. The rules of the law were to pertain to the specific location, lifestyle and situation of the people of Israel. In our day most of the commandments in the Law of Moses are impossible to keep because the context that the law had to operate in (the Temple, Priesthood within the Temple and the Sacrificial System) no longer exists. Based on the scriptures below, if anyone does not keep even one law, they are guilty of breaking the whole law and are under a curse.

> *For whoever keeps the whole law and yet stumbles at just one point is guilty of breaking all of it. James 2:10*

> *For all who rely on the works of the law are under a curse, as it is written: "Cursed is everyone who does not continue to do everything written in the Book of the Law." Clearly no one who relies on the law is justified before God, because "the righteous will live by faith." The law is not based on faith. Galatians 3:10-12a*

With this in mind, let's ask five questions: Who, What, When, Where and Why?

WHO was the law given to? The law was given to Moses for the instruction of the nation of Israel. He obediently wrote in a book the words of the law from the beginning to the end:

> *The LORD said to Moses, "Come up to Me on the mountain and stay here, and I will give you the tablets of stone, with the law and commandments I have written for their instruction. Exodus 24:12*

> *After Moses finished writing in a book the words of this law from beginning to end, he gave this command to the Levites who carried the ark of the covenant of the Lord: "Take this Book of the Law and place it beside the ark of the covenant of the Lord your God. There it will remain as a witness against you." Deuteronomy 31:24-26*

> *These are the statutes and judgments and laws which the Lord made between Himself and the children of Israel on Mount Sinai by the hand of Moses. Leviticus 26:45 NKJV*

FOR WHOM was it given? The law was given for the Israelites as they left Egypt and were about to enter the land of their inheritance:

Now Israel, hear the decrees and laws I am about to teach you. This is the law Moses set before the Israelites. These are the stipulations, decrees and laws Moses gave them when they came out of Egypt. Deuteronomy 4:1a, 44-45

The law was given *only* to the nation of Israel to teach them God's righteous decrees. The law was not for the pagan nations. Out of all nations, only Israel served a living God who was near to them.

What other nation is so great as to have their gods near them the way the LORD our God is near us whenever we pray to Him? And what other nation is so great as to have such righteous decrees and laws as this body of laws I am setting before you today. Deuteronomy 4:7-8

WHAT was the law? The law was their life. It was their "constitution" which contained rules and regulations to live by which anticipated the many situations the people would encounter as they entered the land of their inheritance. These laws provided Israel with knowledge of good and evil as well as rules and regulations that covered all aspects of life. There were blessings for obedience and punishments for disobedience.

Take to heart all the words I have solemnly declared to you this day so that you may command your children to obey carefully all the words of this law. They are not just idle words for you--they are your life. By them you will live long in the land you are crossing the Jordan to possess. Deuteronomy 32:46-47

Behold, I set before you today a blessing and a curse: the blessing, if you obey the commandments of the Lord your

God which I command you today; and the curse, if you do not obey the commandments of the Lord your God, but turn aside from the way which I command you today, to go after other gods which you have not known. Deuteronomy 11:26-28 NKJV

WHEN and WHERE was the law given? The law was given at Mt. Sinai in the third month (Sivan) after the Israelites left Egypt:

On the first day of the third month after the Israelites left Egypt--on that very day--they came to the Desert of Sinai. After they set out from Rephidim, they entered the Desert of Sinai, and Israel camped there in the desert in front of the mountain. Exodus 19:1-2

A vast multitude of up to 2.5 million people had journeyed in the wilderness guided by the presence of God in a pillar of cloud by day and a pillar of fire by night. God was about to give them their rulebook on how to live as His treasured possession.

Then Moses went up to God, and the Lord called to him from the mountain and said, "This is what you are to say to the descendants of Jacob and what you are to tell the people of Israel: 'You yourselves have seen what I did to Egypt, and how I carried you on eagle's wings and brought you to Myself. Now if you obey Me fully and keep My covenant, then out of all the nations you will be My treasured possession." Exodus 19:3-5a

WHY was the law given? God was establishing a new culture for His people. The law was given to teach the Israelites how to live in their covenantal land as the holy, set apart people of God. God also wanted them, His set apart possession, to be a light and a witness to the Gentiles in the hope that they would turn to Israel's living God and reject their dead, carved images.

> *Now Israel, hear the decrees and laws I am about to teach you. Follow them so that you may live and may go in and take possession of the land that the LORD, the God of your fathers, is giving you. See, I have taught you decrees and laws as the LORD your God commanded me, so that you may follow them in the land you are entering to take possession of it. Observe them carefully, for this will show your wisdom and understanding to the nations, who will hear about all these decrees and say, "Surely this great nation is a wise and understanding people." Deuteronomy 4:1, 5-6*

> *For this is what the Lord has commanded us: "I have made you a light for the Gentiles, that you may bring salvation to the ends of the earth." Acts 13:47*

> *I have revealed and saved and proclaimed--I and not some foreign god among you. You are my witnesses, declares the Lord, that I am God. Isaiah 43:12*

When God gave the Law to Moses for the people, He consistently stated, "I am the Lord" and "I am the Lord who makes you holy." God continually reminded the Israelites of His holiness--His "set-apartness," His "wholly otherness." As His people and representatives on the earth, He demanded that they be holy as well.

> *I am the Lord your God; consecrate yourselves and be holy, because I am holy. Leviticus 11:44*

The Israelites had just left a pagan land, Egypt, and they were about to enter another pagan land, Canaan. The Lord did not want His people to follow any of the detestable customs of the peoples living in Egypt or Canaan (Leviticus 18:30). He wanted His holy people to live in His holy land, and the rules were given to separate them *and* the land from the detestable practices of the pagans.

This was how the sovereign Lord determined that His people could dwell in His midst. All this was taking place 1400 years before Jesus' birth, death and resurrection. But now:

> *But now a righteousness from God,* **apart from law,** *has been made known, to which the Law and the Prophets testify. This righteousness from God comes through faith in Jesus Christ to all who believe. Romans 3:21-22a*

Notes

CHAPTER SEVEN
And I Will Give You Rest

Sabbath Rest

God instituted the Sabbath in the second chapter of the book of Genesis. The work of our Creator was completed on the sixth day and on the seventh day He rested from His work. The Hebrew word for rested is *sabat*, which means, "to rest," "to stop or cease from work." God then blessed and sanctified the seventh day because on it He rested from all His work.

> *God saw all that He had made and it was very good. And there was evening, and there was morning—the sixth day. Thus the heavens and the earth were completed in all their vast array. By the seventh day God had finished the work He had been doing; so on the seventh day He rested from all His work. Then God blessed the seventh day and made it holy, because on it He rested from all the work of creating that He had done. Genesis 1:31; 2:1-2*

It was not as though God was tired and needed the rest. As it says in Isaiah 40:28, "The Creator of the ends of the earth will not grow tired or weary." He used the precedent of His rest on the seventh day of creation to establish the principle of Sabbath rest for His people.

> *Remember the Sabbath day by keeping it holy. Six days you shall labor and do all your work, but the seventh day is a Sabbath to the Lord your God. On it you shall not do any work...For in six days the Lord made the heavens and the earth, the sea, and all that is in them, but He rested on the seventh day. Therefore the Lord blessed the Sabbath day and made it holy. Exodus 20:8-11*

We see the principle of Sabbath rest once again when God provided the Israelites manna in the wilderness for only six days and commanded the people to observe the seventh day as the Sabbath. They were told to gather a double portion on the sixth day so that they would have provision and be able to rest on the Sabbath.

> *Bear in mind that the Lord has given you the Sabbath; that is why on the sixth day He gives you bread for two days. Everyone is to stay where they are on the seventh day; no one is to go out. So the people rested on the seventh day. Exodus 16:29-30*

The importance of the Israelites keeping the Sabbath is emphasized when God gave the Sabbath as the sign of the Mosaic covenant between Himself and Israel:

> *The Israelites are to observe the Sabbath, celebrating it for the generations to come as a lasting covenant. It will be a sign between Me and the Israelites forever, for in six days the Lord made the heavens and the earth, and on the seventh day He rested and was refreshed. Exodus 31:16-17*

Observant Jewish people continue to keep the Sabbath to this day, however it has become heavy-laden with rabbinic rules and regulations. Here is a *brief* summary of the basic activities you are required to refrain from in order to become Sabbath observant (shomer Shabbat): writing, erasing, tearing; business transactions; driving or riding in cars or other vehicles; shopping; using the telephone; turning on or off anything which uses electricity, including lights, radios, television, computers, air-conditioners and alarm clocks; cooking, baking or kindling a fire; gardening and grass-mowing; doing laundry.

There are also objects that you are forbidden to move on the Sabbath. These objects are called *Muktzah*. According to Chabad.org, "Muktzah may not be moved directly with one's hand or even indirectly with an object (such as sweeping it away with a broom). However, Muktzah may be moved in a very awkward, unusual manner, with other parts of the body, e.g. with one's teeth or elbow, or by blowing on it. Some categories of Muktzah are: objects which have no designated use, e.g. stones, plants, flowers in a vase, raw food; an object that has broken and become no longer useful such as a broken bowl, a button that falls off; expensive items: camera, crystal decoration; professional tools: scalpel, electric wiring; Important documents: passport, birth certificate."

Do you get the picture of the burden that rules like these place on a person striving to keep the Jewish Sabbath? True Sabbath rest does not mean being burdened with rules and regulations about how to rest! Jesus says, "Come to Me all you who are weary and burdened and *I* will give you rest." (Matthew 11:28)

There were various aspects of the Sabbath that foreshadowed the coming of the Messiah who would provide not only one day of rest, but *permanent* rest for His people. When Moses gave the Law to the people, they had to follow an intricate and labor-intensive set of rules and regulations for six days. After one day of rest, the cycle continued and they would have to labor six more days before they could rest again.

No matter how hard they worked, they could never keep all the laws, so God instituted sacrifices and offerings by which they could be forgiven and restored to relationship with Him. The sacrifices had to be endlessly repeated—a foreshadowing of why the Messiah had to come. Because of His sacrifice, when we put our faith in Him, we no longer have to labor endlessly in order to be righteous before God. We no longer have to strive to please God because Jesus is our permanent Sabbath rest—not just one day a week, but every day of the week.

> *God made Him who had no sin to be sin for us, so that in Him we might become the righteousness of God.*
> *2 Corinthians 5:21*

Jesus taught that what is most important to God is our *heart attitude* toward Him, not the works of the flesh. In Matthew 12:1-14 Jesus tried to expose to some of the Pharisees the condition of their hearts. The Pharisees accused the disciples of breaking the Sabbath law by picking and eating grain as they walked through grain fields on the Sabbath. Jesus began to interpret the true meaning of keeping the Sabbath and told them that HE was Lord of the Sabbath.

> *If you had known what these words mean, 'I desire mercy, not sacrifice,' you would not have condemned the innocent. For the Son of Man is Lord of the Sabbath. Matthew 12:7-8*

Jesus healed a man's hand on the Sabbath and the Pharisees accused Him of breaking the Sabbath law and plotted to kill Him. Once again, Jesus emphasized the importance of the heart attitude.

> *He said to them, "If any of you has a sheep and it falls into a pit on the Sabbath, will you not take hold of it and lift it out? How much more valuable is a man than a sheep! Therefore it is lawful to do good on the Sabbath." Matthew 12:11-12*

Jesus rebuked the Pharisees because they had added a complex and burdensome system of rules, regulations and traditions regarding the Sabbath observance. He asked them,

> *"Why do you break the command of God for the sake of your tradition?" "You hypocrites! Isaiah was right when he prophesied about you: 'These people honor me with their lips, but their hearts are far from Me. They worship Me in vain; their teachings are merely human rules.' Matthew 15:3, 7-9*

God's intent was not to heap Sabbath rules and regulations on the people. His intent was for His people to *rest*. In Mark 2:27 Jesus told the Pharisees: "The

Sabbath was made for man, not man for the Sabbath."

As Lord of the Sabbath, Jesus taught that God gave the Sabbath for man's benefit, and observance of the Sabbath should NOT be characterized by sacrifice (burden) but by mercy (Matthew 12:7). In our day, some people who are returning to their Hebraic roots wonder whether keeping the Sabbath day holy means returning to a strict Jewish observance of the Sabbath. But if you did that, you would not be able to extend mercy to a sick friend who needed you to pick up medicine and groceries on the Sabbath. Keeping the Sabbath day holy does not mean returning to rules and regulations. We have been set free by the blood of Jesus. The Sabbath was instituted for us so that we could rest from our labors, refresh and renew our bodies, and meditate on God's word. What that looks like for each individual is personal. In Jesus, there is grace regarding how we choose to observe, and we are never to judge another's observance.

> *Who are you to judge someone else's servant? To their own master, servants stand or fall. And they will stand, for the Lord is able to make them stand. One person considers one day more sacred than another; another considers every day alike. Each of them should be fully convinced in their own mind. Whoever regards one day as special, does so to the Lord. Whoever eats meat does so to the Lord, for they give thanks to God; and whoever abstains does so to the Lord and gives thanks to God. Romans 14:4-6*

The author of Hebrews explains that *true* rest, *God's* rest, can only be entered into by faith. Many of the

Jewish people rejected the gospel therefore they could never enter God's rest because they did not combine it with faith in the Messiah who was sent to give them true rest.

> *Therefore, since the promise of entering His rest still stands, let us be careful that none of you be found to have fallen short of it. For we also have had the good news proclaimed to us, just as they did; but the message they heard was of no value to them, because they did not share the faith of those who obeyed. Now we who have believed enter that rest, just as God has said, "So I declared on oath in My anger, 'They shall never enter My rest.'"* Hebrews 4:1-3a

David Wilkerson writes, "Scripture makes it clear: The evidence of faith is rest." (David Wilkerson Devotions, Thursday, December 20, 2012). It can also be said that the evidence of rest is faith.

Notes

CHAPTER EIGHT
Take My Yoke Upon You

Faith in Jesus sets us free from the yoke of the Law of Moses. When Jesus spoke to me with the words *Come to Me,* He was not only calling me to follow Him; He also wanted to set me free from the yoke of rules and traditions in which I had been raised. He wanted me to understand that it was my *faith* that set me free. I still enjoy many of the beautiful traditions I was raised with, however I do not observe them out of a sense of burden or obligation. I enjoy them with the full knowledge that it is faith alone that justifies, saves and sets me free.

As a child, my favorite festival was Passover. It was a joyous time when my extended family would gather together to celebrate God's deliverance of our ancestors out of the bondage of slavery in Egypt. Each year, through the Seder meal, we would re-enact that very first Passover and remember God's faithfulness to us. Passover is still my favorite festival, but I see it through very different eyes now. The symbolism in the meal points directly to the Messiah and how He sets me free from the bondage of sin. Each time I celebrate the Passover I am overcome with joy and gratitude that

He opened my eyes to the truth—that He is the true Passover Lamb that was slain.

Although we are eternally bound to the Ten Commandments, those of us who are saved by faith in Jesus are not bound to the Law of Moses. In the following verses, Peter and Paul are referring to the Law of Moses.

> *For you know that it was not with perishable things such as silver or gold that you were redeemed from the empty way of life handed down to you from your ancestors, but with the precious blood of Christ, a lamb without blemish or defect. 1 Peter 1:18-19*

> *But now, by dying to what once bound us, we have been released from the law so that we serve in the new way of the Spirit, and not in the old way of the written code. Romans 7:6*

We are justified--declared righteous by God--by our faith in Christ. It is *Jesus' righteousness* in us that allows God to declare us righteous. We should not go *backward* to the law, or as Paul says, "be held prisoners by the law" (Galatians 3:23). The Law of Moses pointed *forward* to the day that Jesus would fulfill, complete and end it.

> *Christ is the culmination of the law so that there may be righteousness for everyone who believes. Romans 10:4*

"The culmination of the law" comes from the Greek *teleios*, meaning "the end, the termination, that by which a thing is finished, the end to which all things relate, the aim, the purpose." For all who believe, the

Law of Moses ended with the death and resurrection of the Messiah because He alone redeems us. He was the aim and purpose of the law. In His perfection, He was the only one who could fulfill all its requirements. When we put our faith in Him, believers are no longer held prisoner under the yoke of the law. We are freed to live with Jesus' easy yoke of faith. Jesus fulfilled it all. It is that simple.

The Gospel Is For All People

The Law of Moses was given to a specific people, at a specific time and place and for a specific purpose (See chapter 6). God's redemptive plan, however, has always been and will always be for *all people*--Jew and Gentile. In the Book of Genesis, God spoke the gospel to Abraham, "All peoples on earth will be blessed through you" (Genesis 12:3).

> *Scripture foresaw that God would justify the Gentiles by faith, and announced the gospel in advance to Abraham: "All nations will be blessed through you." Galatians 3:8*

When God spoke the gospel to Abraham, only Gentiles lived on the earth. Abraham himself was a Gentile when God first approached him. The blessing to Gentiles was that they would be justified through faith in the Messiah—the Son of David, the Lion of the tribe of Judah--who came through the descendants of Abraham, Isaac and Jacob.

The Great Commission, given to Jesus' disciples, commanded that the gospel go forth to *all creation*. It was the gospel, not the law, which was intended for the Gentiles.

> *He said to them, "Go into all the world and preach the gospel to all creation. Whoever believes and is baptized will be saved, but whoever does not believe will be condemned." Mark 16:15-16*

Gentiles and the Law of Moses

As an apostle commissioned to the Gentiles, Paul continuously spoke about faith vs. the Law of Moses. On his first missionary journey, Paul arrived in Antioch with Barnabas. They went into the synagogue on the Sabbath and began to preach the gospel to both Jews and Gentile proselytes. Paul was very clear that it is faith alone that justifies Jew and Gentile, *not* the Law of Moses.

> *Therefore, my friends, I want you to know that through Jesus the forgiveness of sins is proclaimed to you. Through Him everyone who believes is set free from every sin, a justification you were not able to obtain under the Law of Moses. Acts 13:38-39*

In the 15th chapter of Acts, there occurred a theological milestone in the history of the Church. At the time there were some Jewish believers called Judaizers who believed that in addition to faith in Jesus, Gentiles must be circumcised and observe the Law of Moses—in other words, Gentiles must first convert to Judaism before being eligible for salvation through faith. There was precedent for their reasoning. For generations before the advent of Jesus, Gentiles who wanted to convert to Judaism and worship the God of Israel first had to be circumcised and follow the Law of Moses. There was much dispute over this issue—did Gentiles first have to convert to Judaism in order to be saved? The Jerusalem Council met to settle the dispute. Their answer was clear and unequivocal: NO!

> *The apostles and elders met to consider this question. After much discussion, Peter got up and addressed them: "Brothers, you know that some time ago God made a choice among you that the Gentiles might hear from my lips the message of the gospel and believe. God, who knows the heart, showed that He accepted them by giving the Holy Spirit to them, just as He did to us. He did not discriminate between us and them, for He purified their hearts by faith. Now then, why do you try to test God by putting on the necks of the Gentiles a yoke that neither we nor our ancestors have been able to bear? No! We believe it is through the grace of our Lord Jesus that we are saved, just as they are." Acts 15:6-11*

In Acts 15:19, James declares, "It is my judgment, therefore, that we should not make it difficult for the Gentiles who are turning to God." As a result, there were four stipulations placed on Gentiles at the Jerusalem Council:

1. Abstain from food polluted by idols
2. Abstain from sexual immorality
3. Abstain from the meat of strangled animals
4. Abstain from the blood of animals

These decisions were made by men, chosen by God, and inspired by the Holy Spirit. The gospel is clear—it is by faith through grace that we are saved. As Peter says, putting ourselves under the Law of Moses is a *yoke* that neither Jew nor Gentile can bear. Notice also that Peter says in Acts 15:10 that we *test* God by putting anyone under the Law of Moses. We do not *please* God by adding to our faith, we *test* God--we tempt and provoke Him. The scripture tells us that by testing God in the wilderness, the Israelites were treating Him with contempt:

> *Nevertheless, as surely as I live and as surely as the glory of the LORD fills the whole earth, not one of those who saw My glory and the signs I performed in Egypt and in the wilderness but who disobeyed Me and* tested *Me ten times—not one of them will ever see the land I promised on oath to their ancestors. No one who has treated Me with contempt will ever see it. Numbers 14:21-23*

When we add anything to faith, it tests, tempts, provokes and treats God with contempt. This alone should put the fear of God in us and should not be taken lightly. When we add anything to faith, we also place a yoke upon ourselves that we simply cannot bear.

Notes

CHAPTER NINE
Only a Shadow

As we read a book, starting at the beginning and reading forward to the end, the story develops. As the plot progresses, more is revealed; more definition and clarity come into focus. Things that were only a shadow begin to come to light. So it is with the bible. If you start reading the bible at the gospels, you lose the context of the first two-thirds of its message. Conversely, it is problematic when you don't realize that as you move from the Old Testament into the New, the story progresses—more is clarified and revealed. Things that were mere shadows become clearer and more defined. I believe that God's word is to be read and understood as a book—beginning with Genesis and allowing the story to develop and unfold as it moves into the gospels, the epistles and the Book of Revelation.

A shadow is an image cast by an object that comes between light and a surface. It represents the form of the object as opposed to the actual object itself. A shadow is without substance. It is defined as "an area of *darkness* created when a source of *light* is blocked; a very small amount of something." With this in mind, scripture tells us that the Law of Moses, the Old Covenant given to the Israelites at Sinai, is only a shadow, but the substance is Jesus.

> *The law is only a shadow of the good things that are coming—not the realities themselves. For this reason it can never, by the same sacrifices repeated endlessly year after year, make perfect those who draw near to worship. Hebrews 10:1*

> *So let no one judge you in food or in drink, or regarding a festival, or a new moon or Sabbaths, which are a shadow of the things to come; but the substance is of Christ. Colossians 2:16-17 NKJV*

These next verses speak of a superior new covenant established on better promises:

> *Now the main point of what we are saying is this: We do have such a High Priest, who sat down at the right hand of the throne of the Majesty in heaven, and who serves in the sanctuary, the true tabernacle set up by the Lord, not by a mere human being. Every high priest is appointed to offer both gifts and sacrifices, and so it was necessary for this one also to have something to offer. If He were on earth, He would not be a priest, for there are already priests who offer the gifts prescribed by the law. They serve at a sanctuary that is a copy and shadow of what is in heaven. But in fact the ministry Jesus has received is as superior to theirs as the covenant of which He is Mediator is superior to the old one, since the new covenant is established on better promises. For if there had been nothing wrong with that first covenant, no place would have been sought for another. Hebrews 8:1-5a, 6-7*

The first covenant (Law of Moses/Old Covenant) was only meant to be a copy and shadow pointing to the New Covenant in Jesus' blood. Jesus *is* the light and He came and dwelt among us. When He did, there was no longer a shadow because the light had come. According to Hebrews 8:13, the New Covenant makes the Old Covenant obsolete and outdated:

> *By calling this covenant "new," He has made the first one obsolete, and what is obsolete and outdated will soon disappear.*

It is not as though a perfect God made a mistake when He gave the Old (Mosaic) Covenant. The problem was not with the covenant, but that the people could never keep the covenant. The Mosaic covenant was the only covenant given to Israel that was not eternal. It was a shadow of the "far better" covenant (the New Covenant in Jesus' blood) that would be eternal and would be available to all through faith. The other three covenants given to Israel (Abrahamic, Davidic and New) were eternal covenants based on eternal promises.

After the covenants given to Adam and Noah, the Gentiles were never again given a covenant until the New Covenant in Jesus' blood was made available to them through faith. The Law of Moses, the Mosaic Covenant, was given to Israel alone. But the glorious New Covenant in Jesus' blood is offered to both Jew and Gentile through faith. Before the New Covenant, Gentiles were separate from Christ, excluded from citizenship in Israel, and foreigners to the covenants of promise given to Israel. But, in Jesus, Gentiles are now fellow citizens with Israel in God's kingdom—one new man.

> *Remember that at that time you were separate from Christ, excluded from citizenship in Israel and foreigners to the covenants of the promise, without hope and without God in the world. But now in Christ Jesus you who were once far away have been brought near through the blood of Christ. Consequently, you are no longer foreigners and strangers, but fellow citizens with God's people, built on the foundation of the apostles and prophets, with Christ Jesus Himself as the chief cornerstone. Ephesians 2:12-13, 19-20*

As God's story unfolds, we see the need for a New Covenant in Jesus' blood that would atone for sin once for all and that would include *all* who believe. Nowhere does Paul say that in Jesus Gentiles are under the Law of Moses. We move ***forward*** into the New Covenant. We would be moving ***backward*** if we went into the shadow of the Old. Jesus is the substance of the shadow.

Notes

CHAPTER TEN

Learn from Me

The Higher Law

Jesus consistently pointed out that what was most important to God was not the literal works of the Law but the *heart* motivation—The Law of Love—the higher law. He continuously differentiated between the *spirit* of the law (the heart motivation) and the *letter* of the law (literal works).

> *"Teacher, which is the greatest commandment in the Law?" Jesus replied: "'Love the Lord your God with all your heart and with all your soul and with all your mind.' This is the first and greatest Commandment. And the second is like it: 'Love your neighbor as yourself.' All the Law and the Prophets hang on these two commandments.' Matthew 22:36-40*

These two laws—love for God and love for one another summarize God's eternal Ten Commandments. Jesus frees us from the bondage of the commandments contained in the Law of Moses. He simply calls us to love God and one another. This Law of Love, summed up in the Great Commandment—to love God and one another--is what believers in Jesus are called to follow.

When we do, we are fulfilling everything God requires of us. Loving God does not mean following a list of burdensome commands that we can check off. Jesus asked Peter three times if he loved Him and three times Jesus explained to Peter what it meant to love Him: "Feed My lambs", "Take care of My sheep", "Feed My sheep" (John 21:15-17). In other words, love one another. James calls it the Royal Law.

> *If you really keep the royal law found in Scripture, "Love your neighbor as yourself," you are doing right.*
> *James 2:8*

Jesus beautifully illustrated the *spirit* of the law of loving one's neighbor in the parable of the Good Samaritan (Luke 10:25-37). A man wounded by robbers lay nearly dead in the road. A Jewish priest and a Levite came down the road but passed by the man on the other side of the road, because they did not know if the man was dead or alive. They were obeying the *letter* of the law that commanded, "Do not defile yourself by going near a dead body." But when a Samaritan walking down the road saw the wounded man, he went to him, bandaged his wounds, took him to an inn and paid the innkeeper to care for the man. Jesus asked, "Which of these three do you think was a neighbor to the man who fell into the hands of robbers?" An expert in the law replied, "The one who had mercy on him." "Go and do likewise," Jesus replied.

Jesus challenges us to love the unlovely—to love our enemies, to do good to those who hate us, to bless those who curse us, and to pray for those who mistreat us (Luke 6:27-28). He calls us to imitate God by being merciful just as our Father is merciful (Luke 6:36).

And if you do good to those who are good to you, what credit is that to you? Even sinners do that. And if you lend to those from whom you expect repayment, what credit is that to you? Even sinners lend to sinners, expecting to be repaid in full. But love your enemies, do good to them, and lend to them without expecting to get anything back. Luke 6:34-35a

Paul confirms Jesus' Law of Love in 1 Corinthians as he speaks of love as the "most excellent way".

And yet I will show you the most excellent way. Love is patient, love is kind. It does not envy, it does not boast, it is not proud. It does not dishonor others, it is not self-seeking, it is not easily angered, it keeps no record of wrongs. Love does not delight in evil but rejoices with the truth. It always protects, always trusts, always perseveres. 1 Corinthians 12:31b; 13:4-7

God is eternal and God is love, therefore love is eternal. Even the most powerful and magnificent manifestations of the Spirit are meaningless unless they are manifested *in love*. All that will remain as we stand before God is how well we loved Him and how well we loved one another.

As I think back on my own testimony, it was the power of the women's love for Jesus and for me that drew me like a magnet straight to His heart. Love never fails. When we have the love of Jesus in us and express that to one another, there is nothing more powerful or more pleasing to God. If the Body of Messiah would really tap into the depth of the Father's love for us, and express that love back to Him and to one another, this world would be a very different place.

Clean and Unclean

Jesus once again emphasized the spirit of the law versus the letter of the law in Mark 7. The Pharisees and some teachers of the law saw some of Jesus' disciples eating food with unwashed hands. Their *tradition* was that all Jews must ceremonially wash their hands before eating. They asked Jesus, "Why don't your disciples live according to the *tradition* of the elders instead of eating their food with 'unclean' hands?" (Mark 7:5) Jesus replied:

> *"You have let go of the commands of God and are holding on to* human traditions. *You have a fine way of setting aside the commands of God in order to observe your own traditions!" Again Jesus called the crowd to Him and said, "Listen to Me, everyone, and understand this. Nothing outside a person can defile them by going into them. Rather, it is what comes out of a person that defiles them." Mark 7:8-9, 14-16*

> *After He had left the crowd and entered the house, His disciples asked Him about this parable. "Are you so dull?" He asked. "Don't you see that nothing that enters a person from the outside can defile them? For it doesn't go into their heart but into their stomach, and then out of the body."* (In saying this, Jesus declared all foods clean.) *Mark 7:17-19*

Fifteen hundred years after the law was given, Jesus addressed what had become of the law.

It had evolved into rules, regulations and the traditions of man. He taught His disciples the spirit of the law—it is the *heart* motivation that matters to God. It is not what goes into a person's stomach that makes them clean, it is what comes out of the heart that determines cleanliness. No *food* can contaminate a person's heart.

Who Has Bewitched You?

In his epistle to the Galatians, Paul expresses his frustration. False teaching was entering the churches in the province of Galatia. The false teaching: Gentiles must observe the law *in addition to* their faith in Jesus. This was in direct contradiction to Paul's teaching that salvation was by grace through faith alone. Listen to the frustration in Paul's words:

> *You foolish Galatians! Who has bewitched you? Before your very eyes Jesus Christ was clearly portrayed as crucified. I would like to learn just one thing from you: Did you receive the Spirit by works of the law, or by believing what you heard? Are you so foolish? After beginning by means of the Spirit, are you now trying to finish by means of the flesh? Galatians 3:1-3*

In other words, "Who has cast a spell on you?" "Who has hypnotized you?" "Who has led you into evil doctrine?" The Galatians began rightly with the Spirit revealing Christ to them. But they were being strongly influenced by false teaching and were reverting backwards, trying to obtain righteousness by works of the law. As Paul says in the following verses, if you put yourself back under the law, you have alienated yourself from Christ and have fallen away from grace. These stern cautions have applied throughout the ages and still apply today. It would be foolhardy not to take them seriously. The law and grace are mutually exclusive; they cannot co-exist.

> *It is for freedom that Christ has set us free. Stand firm, then, and do not let yourselves be burdened again by a yoke of slavery. Mark my words! I, Paul, tell you that if you let yourselves be circumcised, Christ will be of no value to you at all. Again I declare to every man who lets himself be circumcised that he is obligated to obey the whole law. You who are trying to be justified by the law have been alienated from Christ; you have fallen away from grace. Galatians 5:1-4*

These are strong words from Paul and he couldn't be any clearer—Jesus is of no value to those trying to obtain righteousness through the works of the law. And who knew better than Paul, a Hebrew of Hebrews, who had been there and done it all regarding the law and he called it all *garbage*.

> *If someone thinks they have reasons to put confidence in the flesh, I have more: circumcised on the eighth day, of the people of Israel, of the tribe of Benjamin, a Hebrew of Hebrews in regard to the law, a Pharisee; as for zeal, persecuting the church; as for righteousness based on the law, faultless. But whatever were gains to me I now consider loss for the sake of Christ. What is more, I consider*

everything a loss because of the surpassing worth of knowing Christ Jesus my Lord, for whose sake I have lost all things. I consider them garbage, that I may gain Christ and be found in Him, not having a righteousness of my own that comes from the law, but that which is through faith in Christ—the righteousness that comes from God on the basis of faith. Philippians 3:4b-9

Paul is consistent in his writings regarding the Law of Moses, and those who believe it is *necessary* to follow the law would be contradicting Paul's message. He continues to point out that the law could never accomplish what only the work of redemption on the cross did accomplish.

When you were dead in your sins and in the uncircumcision of your flesh, God made you alive with Christ. He forgave us all our sins, having canceled the charge of our legal indebtedness, which stood against us and condemned us; He has taken it away, nailing it to the cross. Colossians 2:13-14

What Paul is saying is, "It's done!" "It's finished!" "It was nailed to the cross!" What did Jesus say at the cross?

When He had received the drink, Jesus said, "It is finished!" With that, He bowed His head and gave up His spirit. John 19:30

The Law of Moses is finished for those in Jesus. Our debt was paid for at the cross. If we believe we become more righteous by doing any of the works of the law, we negate all the work accomplished at the cross.

Notes

CHAPTER ELEVEN

My Yoke is Easy and My Burden is Light

Freedom at the Cross

On this side of heaven, I'm not sure we can fully fathom all that was accomplished at the cross. But one common theme throughout the New Testament is freedom. Not the freedom to sin, but freedom from the burden of rules and regulations. In Jesus we are freed from the penalty that sin and death bring. Freedom is a consistent theme in Paul's epistles. Paul knew only too well the burden of rules and regulations that the law produced, and by God's grace he was set free. Paul was called, set apart and given special revelation that has been passed down for all of us. The revelation given to Paul and written down for us is a gift from God, and God desires that we walk in the freedom that His Son's sacrifice offers us. It is for freedom's sake that Jesus has set us free from the law (Galatians 5:1). Otherwise Jesus died in vain.

> *The life I live in the body, I live by faith in the Son of God, who loved me and gave Himself for me. I do not set aside the grace of God, for if righteousness could be gained through the law, Christ died for nothing! Galatians 2:20b-21*

Paul explains that those who live under the Law of Moses have a veil upon their hearts and minds. The veil can only be removed and freedom can only come when one puts their faith in Jesus.

> *Even to this day when Moses is read, a veil covers their hearts. But whenever anyone turns to the Lord, the veil is taken away. Now the Lord is the Spirit, and where the Spirit of the Lord is, there is freedom. And we all, who with unveiled faces contemplate the Lord's glory, are being transformed into His image with ever-increasing glory, which comes from the Lord who is the Spirit.*
> 2 Corinthians 3:15-18

The simple truth: When we are yoked with Jesus, He carries the load and we are no longer burdened. Our freedom comes from the fact that our righteousness doesn't come from the law, but from Jesus' sacrifice on the cross. Jesus Himself tells us that He has set us *free* indeed (John 8:36). He is the mediator of a new covenant that sets us *free* from the sins committed under the Old Covenant (Hebrews 9:15). In Him we can approach a holy God with *freedom* and confidence (Ephesians 3:12). The law we now follow is a *perfect* law that gives us *freedom* (James 1:25).

Jesus Reigns Supreme

The book of Hebrews was written to a Jewish believing audience that was being tempted to return to the Law of Moses. The theme of Hebrews is the absolute supremacy of Jesus. The two Greek words for "better" (kreitton) and "superior" (diaphoros) are used 15 times in the book of Hebrews. The author points out the overwhelming superiority of Jesus over anything the Law offered. He reveals Jesus' supremacy over the Prophets (1:1-3); His supremacy over the angels (1:4-2:8); His supremacy over Moses (3:1-19); over Joshua (4:1-13); over Aaron's priesthood (4:14-7:18); and His supremacy over the entire ritual contained within the law (7:19-10:39).

> *In the past God spoke to our ancestors through the prophets at many times and in various ways, but in these last days He has spoken to us by His Son, whom He appointed Heir of all things, and through whom also He made the universe. The Son is the radiance of God's glory and the exact representation of His being, sustaining all things by His powerful word. After He had provided purification for sins, He sat down at the right hand of the Majesty in heaven. Hebrews 1:1-3*

Nothing can surpass Him. Nothing even comes close—not the angels, not the prophets, not the Levitical priesthood, and certainly not the Law of Moses. The author of Hebrews confirms that the new covenant in Jesus' blood sets us free from the law.

> *How much more, then, will the blood of Christ, who through the eternal Spirit offered Himself unblemished to God, cleanse our consciences from acts that lead to death, so that we may serve the living God! For this reason Christ is the mediator of a new covenant, that those who are called may receive the promised eternal inheritance—now that He has died as a ransom to set them*

free from the sins committed under the first covenant. Hebrews 9:14-15

Back to the Beginning

It is enriching to understand the Jewish roots of the faith, but for those who are seeking to find their identity there, perhaps they believe that by doing this they are going back to the beginnings of their faith—back to Abraham—but they aren't going back far enough. Look at what Jesus says to His Jewish brethren and to all of us:

Your father Abraham rejoiced at the thought of seeing My day; he saw it and was glad. "Very truly I tell you," Jesus answered, "before Abraham was born, I AM!" John 8:56, 58

Jesus spoke the words I AM to show that He was One with the Father, and that He was with the Father from the beginning. Jesus made seven I AM statements to show that He eternally existed with the Father. They are recorded in the book of John:

"I AM the bread of life" (6:35)
"I AM the light of the world" (8:12; 9:5)
"I AM the door" (10:7, 9)
"I AM the good shepherd" (10:11,14)
"I AM the resurrection and the life" (11:25)
"I AM the way, the truth, and the life" (14:6)
"I AM the true vine" (15:1, 5)

Jesus is fully God and fully man. As the Nicene Creed states, He is "very God and of very God."

> *In the beginning was the Word and the Word was with God and the Word was God. He was with God in the beginning. Through Him all things were made; without Him nothing was made that has been made. In Him was life, and that life was the light of all mankind. John 1:1-4*
>
> *For in Christ all the fullness of the Deity dwells in bodily form. Colossians 2:9*

The theme of God's story is redemption. Only Jesus, The Lamb of God who is seated at the right hand of the Father, could accomplish that which the Law of Moses was never able to do. With His own blood Jesus purchased men for God from every tribe, language, people and nation. (Revelation 5:9) With the shedding of His blood once for all, the continuous shedding of animal's blood was no longer necessary. God presented Jesus as a sacrifice of atonement through faith in *His* blood. (Romans 3:25) And through His blood, our redemption is found. Jesus is eternal and God's story *begins* and *ends* with Him.

> *Look, I am coming soon! My reward is with Me, and I will give to everyone according to what they have done. I am the Alpha and the Omega, the First and the Last, the Beginning and the End. Revelation 22:12-13*

Our true spiritual and eternal identity is found only in Jesus—we are His Bride. He is our glorious Bridegroom and He is coming back for His Bride. John the Baptist came in the spirit and power of Elijah to make ready for the Lord a people prepared (Luke 1:17). Regardless of whether we are Jew or Gentile, as His

Bride we are to be radiant and without stain or wrinkle or any other blemish (Ephesians 5:27). May we all be found ready at His return.

> *Hallelujah! For our Lord God Almighty reigns. Let us rejoice and be glad and give Him glory! For the wedding of the Lamb has come, and His Bride has made herself ready. Revelation 19:6b, 7*

Notes

CHAPTER TWELVE

How Then Shall We Live—Aligning with God's Heart

Out of the nations God called Abram and Sarai to form a people set apart to Him for His redemptive purposes. He called this people a peculiar treasure above all people (Exodus 19:5). The Hebrew word for peculiar, *segullah*, means "personally acquired", "carefully preserved" and "privately possessed". God has most certainly *carefully preserved* this people with whom He covenanted eternally. Throughout history, despite unbelievable odds, the Jewish people have survived complete annihilation.

Although many Jews have already come to know their Messiah, scripture tells us in Romans 11 that *all Israel* will come to salvation at the fullness of the Gentiles, which will coincide with Jesus' return.

> *For I do not desire, brethren, that you should be ignorant of this mystery, lest you should be wise in your own opinion, that blindness in part has happened to Israel until the fullness of the Gentiles has come in. And so all Israel will be saved, as it is written: "The Deliverer will come out of Zion, and He will turn away ungodliness from Jacob; For this is My*

covenant with them, when I take away their sins."
Romans 11:25-27 NKJV

The "fullness of the Gentiles" not only refers to all those who will be saved among the Gentiles, but also to the "spiritual fullness" or "spiritual maturity" of the Gentiles. Spiritual fullness/maturity does not mean that Gentiles are to take on a Jewish identity. Spiritual maturity means embracing who you were created to be, having confidence that in the Messiah you are a son or daughter of God. Gentile believers become part of God's family along with the Jewish people, and this is beautifully expressed in our "one new man" identity. It is good that God made both Jew and Gentile, each with a distinct role. It is *God's* plan and it is a perfect and beautiful plan.

With the revelation that in Messiah they are part of God's family along with their Jewish brothers and sisters, what can Gentiles do to align with God's will? As the nations rage against Israel and the Jewish people in our day and as anti-Semitism is rising at an alarming rate, believers are not to stand by and do nothing. A Gentile voice, boldly proclaiming love and support for Israel, needs to cry out throughout the earth. A warning from the prophet Obadiah:

> *On the day you stood aloof while strangers carried off his wealth and foreigners entered his gates and cast lots for Jerusalem,* you were like one of them. *Obadiah 1:11*

To idly stand by while the world comes against Israel *is to be like them.* "Evil flourishes when good men do nothing." (Edmund Burke)

God told the prophet Isaiah to comfort His people Israel in the midst of their suffering. Gentile believers are also called to speak tender words of comfort to the Jewish people.

> *Comfort, comfort My people, says your God. Speak tenderly to Jerusalem and proclaim to her that her hard service has been completed, that her sin has been paid for, that she has received from the Lord's hand double for all her sins. Isaiah 40:1-2*

Pray, pray, pray!

We also agree with God's will by crying out day and night for the salvation of Israel. Pray that the Body of Messiah becomes burdened to never be silent until Jerusalem shines brightly.

> *For Zion's sake, I will not keep silent, for Jerusalem's sake I will not remain quiet, till her vindication shines out like the dawn, her salvation like a blazing torch. Isaiah 62:1*

> *I have posted watchmen on your walls, Jerusalem; they will never be silent day or night. You who call on the Lord, give yourselves no rest, and give Him no rest till he establishes Jerusalem and makes her the praise of the earth. Isaiah 62:6-7*

Pray that the wind of the Spirit will tear the veil that lies over the hearts of the Jewish people in Israel and throughout the Diaspora (2 Corinthians 3:15).

Pray for the peace, security and prosperity of Jerusalem. There is a day coming when *all* nations will fight against Jerusalem (Zechariah 14:2).

> *Pray for the peace of Jerusalem: "May those who love you be secure. May there be peace within your walls and security within your citadels." For the sake of my brothers and friends, I will say, "Peace be within you." For the sake of the house of the Lord our God, I will seek your prosperity. Psalm 122:6-9*

Intercede that our nation will not turn its back on Israel. Pray that a spirit of repentance would fall upon those in our nation who have not endorsed God's will to unabashedly stand with Israel. As we bless Israel, we will be blessed. (Genesis 12:3)

Pray that the remnant of Jewish believers throughout the world will be strengthened, encouraged and supported by their Gentile brothers and sisters. Pray also for the "one new man" reality to be manifest in Jewish and Gentile believers.

When we walk in the confidence of our identity in Jesus, we are able to embrace with joy and gratitude who God created us to be—whether Jew or Gentile. This is the spirit of Sonship. This is who we were created to be—sons and daughters of the living God. Nothing surpasses that and nothing surpasses Him.

> *Oh, the depth of the riches of the wisdom and knowledge of God! How unsearchable His judgments, and His paths beyond tracing out! Who has known the mind of the Lord? Or who has been His counselor? Who has ever given to God, that God should repay him? For from Him and through Him and for Him are all things. To Him be the glory forever. Amen. Romans 11:33-36*

Notes